RABBITS

From Hares and Jackrabbits
to Adorable Pets

RABBITS

From Hares and Jackrabbits
to Adorable Pets

TOM JACKSON

amber
BOOKS

Published by Amber Books Ltd
United House
North Road
London
N7 9DP
United Kingdom
www.amberbooks.co.uk
Instagram: amberbooksltd
Facebook: amberbooks
Twitter: @amberbooks
Pinterest: amberbooksltd

ISBN: 978-1-83886-370-8

Project Editor: Michael Spilling
Designer: Keren Harragan
Picture Research: Adam Gnych

Printed in China

Contents

Introduction

A simple creature with a distinctive look, rabbits have many sides to their character. For many of us, it is one of the few truly wild mammals we see regularly. Our intensively developed countrysides have pushed out many native species, and the ever-adaptable rabbit is largely all that remains. We see them in our vehicle headlights at night, gambolling on the edges of a woodland at dusk and running wild in spring – although it could be hares or jackrabbits we are seeing.

However, this wildness belies another important feature of rabbits: they make great pets. Wild rabbits are social creatures and so domestic life among a human family is not too far removed from a natural existence. We humans have not held back with our love for rabbits. There are hundreds of artificial breeds, each with a cute look and character to choose from.

And yet, there is another role that the rabbit plays, one of destruction and damage. In cahoots with human settlers spreading across the globe, the European rabbit has travelled too, first as a food animal but soon running feral. For the last 250 years, sleek rabbits, unfussy over habitat or diet, used their hyper-efficient reproductive system to populate new lands. This has happened most notably in Australia and New Zealand, where the rabbit has forced out native species and been a direct cause of multiple extinctions. The story of pest rabbit control is littered with wrong turns, but the process continues. Rabbits are, indeed, a cute marvel of evolution that makes them both ordinary and extraordinary.

OPPOSITE:

Cottontail
There are dozens of species of rabbit living across the world, such as the cottontail from the broad-leaf woodlands of North America. All rabbits have long ears and bounding legs, but subtle differences in behaviour can have big effects on life in the wild and in the home.

Rabbit Breeds

Rabbits may not be able to compete with cats and dogs for a place in the family home, but they are a clear favourite for third place in the competition for being our furry friends. In many ways pet rabbits are less demanding than their carnivorous rivals, being content with grass and the odd salad vegetable (including carrots). Nevertheless they come with some drawbacks. Rabbits like company so where there is one, there really should be two or three. Additionally, they must dig and nibble, but not to annoy; its important for their overall health. So putative rabbit owners need to have the space and a strategy for their pet to live as a rabbit should.

There are a little more than 300 officially recognized breeds of domestic rabbit, and hundreds more are being developed. All are descendants of the wild European rabbit species, *Oryctolagus cuniculus*. The breeds do not all have their roots in the pet trade. Rabbits were originally domesticated as a food animal, and meat breeds are longer and more robust than the compact bunnies that have been bred to live out their days as cuddly companions. Rabbits were also traditionally an inexpensive source of fur and fine wool. The fluffy long-haired breeds are now a favourite of animals kept for show, but be warned, their floaty locks require considerable care and attention.

OPPOSITE:
Dutch rabbit
Despite the name, this dwarf breed has its origins in England and Belgium, yet has its most dominant base today in North America. American Dutch rabbits have a saddle, where the shoulders and forebody are white and the back and rump is darker.

Kits

Young rabbits are perhaps better known as bunnies, but the more formal term is 'kit' or 'kitten'. These kits have a tortoiseshell fur colouring.

LEFT TOP:
Rabbit wool
The long, fine hairs of the Angora breed can be spun into the finest wool yarns, much prized for being softer and silkier than sheep's wool. Angora breeds hail from Turkey originally but have been diversified into many breeds across Europe.

LEFT BOTTOM AND OPPOSITE:
French Angora
At about 4.5kg (10lb) when fully grown, this medium-sized Angora breed differs from the rest in that its face and feet have short fur; this helps them stay clean and healthy while the dense woolly coat grows elsewhere.

Wide appeal
Although Angora rabbits were
initially bred for their wool,
they have great appeal as a show
breed and as a pet. However,
their long hairs require a lot
of attention to maintain the
signature look.

ALL PHOTOGRAPHS:
Gotland rabbit
This athletic breed represents the ancestors of the Swedish farm rabbit, which were extensively raised for their meat and skins until the 20th century. Today, domestic rabbits are much less common and the Gotland breed is classified as endangered.

Jersey Wooly
This breed is named after the US state of New Jersey, where it was first produced in the late 1980s. The aim was to make a cute and cuddly breed with long, soft hair that is easy to maintain. The ideal weight of the compact Jersey Wooly breed is around 1.25kg (2.75lb). The breed has Angora in its ancestry but by crossing with dwarf and chinchilla breeds the fine hairs have been shortened, thickened and reduced in density. The long-haired breed therefore requires only minimum care to stay in good condition.

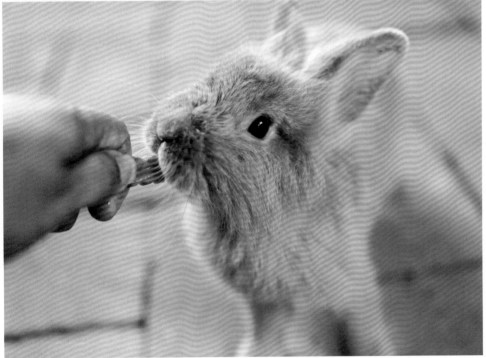

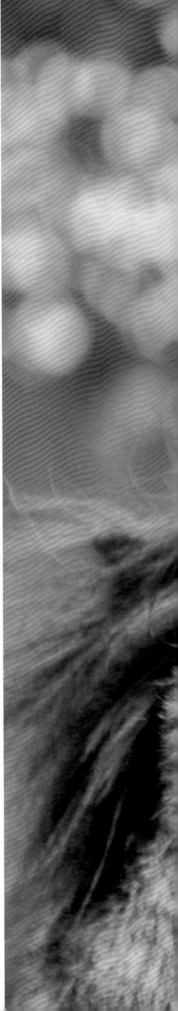

ALL PHOTOGRAPHS:
Lionhead
One of the newest breeds, this Belgian variety was only officially recognized in 2002 – and in 2014 in North America. It was bred from a cross between the Jersey Wooly and the Netherland Dwarf. It is named after the distinctive 'mane' of long hairs that grow on top of the head and nape. Unlike its feline namesake, this feature is seen in all adults, both bucks and does. Lionhead kits have a shorter haircut in their early days.

ALL PHOTOGRAPHS:

Mini Rex

This American pet breed was created in the mid-1980s in Florida. It uses a mutation first isolated in the 1880s that makes the fur grow out straight from the body rather than lying flat against the skin. The thicker guard hairs, which are usually longer and are the same length as the dense underfur, gives the breed's coat a plush, velvet appearance.

The Mini Rex is a small, or compact, breed, averaging around 2kg (4.4lb) in weight. The compact breeds have an obviously rounded body with the back line rising above the shoulders.

ALL PHOTOGRAPHS:
Pannon White
This medium-to-large breed – weighing in at 4.5kg (10lb) – is not yet
fully recognized by the international breed associations and councils.
It was created in Hungary by crossing white rabbit breeds from New
Zealand and California.

ALL PHOTOGRAPHS:

Satin rabbit

Named for its glossy hair, this American breed was created in the 1950s for both its fur and meat. Today it is a popular contender in rabbit shows, although the albino strain is still bred for its flesh. The silken coat is due to long, soft guard hairs that reflect the light. The 'satin' mutation arose in Havana rabbits in the 1930s.

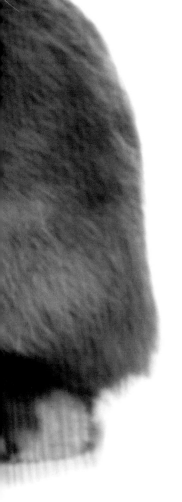

Being a large rabbit with a big appetite and requiring considerable space, the Silver Fox is not well suited to being a pet, Now that the demand for rabbit fur and meat has diminished, this handsome breed is rare and is threatened with being lost.

ALL PHOTOGRAPHS:
Teddy Dwarf
This fluffy little German breed is the product of a cross between a lionhead and an Angora in 2009. The cute look achieved has been a great success, and this as-yet unofficial breed is a popular choice across Europe.

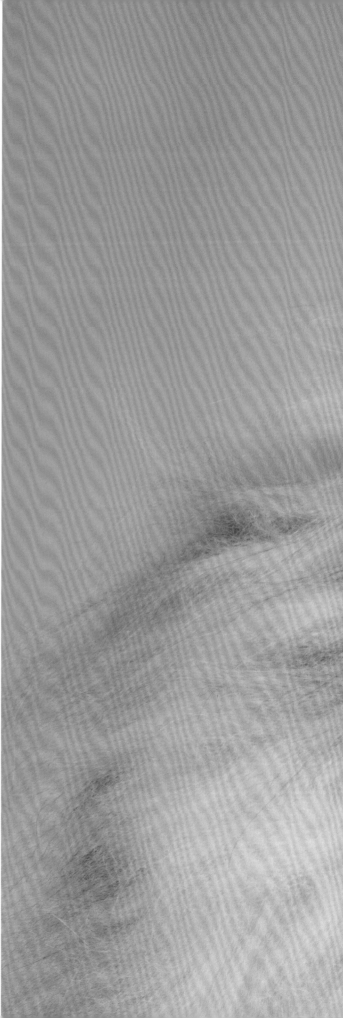

White Vienna
There are numerous breeds of
white rabbits. Notable ones
are the Californian and Florida
White breeds. The White Vienna
is a relatively new addition and
is noteworthy for a mutation
that gives these Austrian rabbits
striking ice-blue eyes. Most
whites have a ruby-pink iris.

Wild Rabbits

There are about 21 species that have the common name 'rabbit'. A confusion may lie in the distinction between rabbits and their larger, rougher and tougher close cousins, hares. It is not always obvious which is which, just by looking at them from afar. Taking a much closer look reveals all. Rabbit species have 44 chromosomes, whereas hares have 48.

As we will see, many wild rabbit species are confined to specific habitats and sometimes almost impossibly small ranges. However, there is one species that rules the world. This is the European rabbit, also referred to simply as the wild rabbit. This is the familiar species that lives in social groups of 20 adults, which work together to dig a network of communal burrows called a warren. This species is originally from the Iberian Peninsula. That name stems from the Roman province of Hispania, which literally means 'land of rabbits'. The Romans spread rabbits across their empire, and latterly, when Europeans colonized other continents, the animals moved too.

These far-flung lands often had their own rabbit species. There are a handful living in Asia, but rabbits do best in temperate areas of woodland and meadow. The Americas have 14 cottontail species. These do not burrow for themselves and are distinguished by the white flash on their tails.

OPPOSITE:
Wild rabbit
This European species is the wild ancestor of all domestic and pet rabbit breeds. Spread out from Spain across Europe by the Romans and then the world by colonial settlers, this is one of the world's most widespread mammals.

Opportunity knocks
The European rabbit was originally adapted for life in mountain woodlands with soft soils, but it has now taken to life in a great range of habitats from rocky deserts to wide open grasslands.

Turn of speed
A determined bird of prey fails to catch a rabbit. The mammal has used its long hind limbs to sprint away to safety. The rabbit can hit a top speed of 40km/h (25mph) over short distances, just enough to get the animal back to the relative safety of its burrow.

ABOVE:
Life underground
European rabbits spend most of the day sleeping underground.
They dig burrows into well-drained soils that will not flood after
heavy rains, and generally live in colonies of about ten adults that
work together to defend their home, the warren.

OPPOSITE:
Amami rabbit
This endangered species lives only on the islands of Amami and
Tokuno in Japan's Okinawa archipelago in the western Pacific.
It is also known as the Ryukyu rabbit. The dark brown species is
thought to be the last remaining descendant of a rabbit species that
once lived across the Asian mainland.

ALL PHOTOGRAPHS:
Pygmy rabbit
This little American species lives in the arid Great Basin of the western United States. It is the only native American lagomorph to dig its own burrow. There is a small isolated population to the north in the basin of the Columbia River, where pygmy rabbits are in decline. A breeding programme is in place for this subgroup and the little rabbits are being steadily reintroduced into the wild.

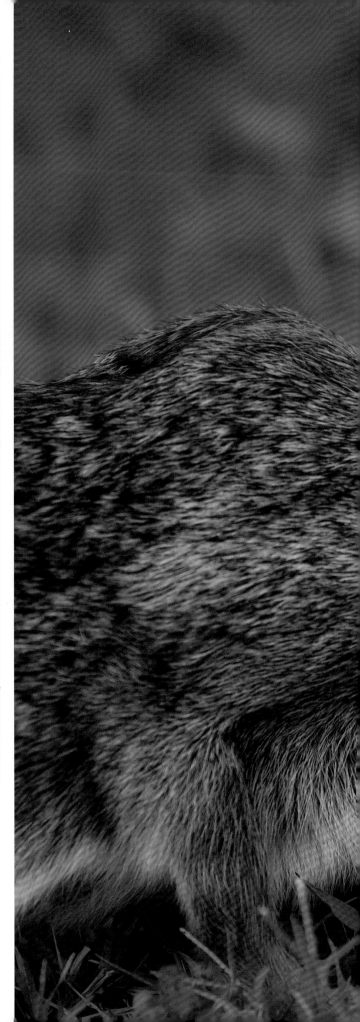

ALL PHOTOGRAPHS:
Cottontails
Most wild species of American rabbits are better known as cottontails, due to the flash of white fur under the tail. This patch is a signal to other rabbits – mostly of danger. There are 14 species of cottontails living from southern Canada to the pampas of Paraguay and Argentina. The forest rabbit, or tapiti, even lives in the southern region of the Amazon rainforest. Cottontails are more common in North America. This one is an eastern cottontail that is found from Central America to Canada. The marsh rabbit is a cottontail that swims in the bayous of the Deep South and the desert cottontail lives in the American West.

LEFT:

Volcano rabbit

This Mexican species is very rare. It lives only on the slopes of two volcanic mountain ranges south of Mexico City. It is thought that about 7000 of these critically endangered rabbits live in the wild, and their mountain habitat is under threat from wildfires and fragmentation due to human developments.

ABOVE TOP AND MIDDLE:

Warren

The network of burrows, known as a warren, is the preserve of European wild rabbits and a few much rarer species that gather in small cooperative groups. The burrows of a warren interconnect with sleeping and nursery chambers deeper down. If a predator – a snake or rat – enters one tunnel, the inhabitants can escape from another.

ABOVE BOTTOM:

Droppings

The small rounded pellets of rabbit droppings are easy to spot. They are used to mark the territory of a warren or a nesting hole of a solitary species.

Riverine rabbit
This nocturnal rabbit from southern Africa is the rarest species of all. There are only 500 adults in the wild. It lives in the lowland scrub of Cape Province, where it hides out from the heat of the day in hollows dug in the shade of shrubs. By night the rabbit comes out to feed, but it is finding it ever harder to find enough wild habitat to survive.

Jackrabbits, Hares & Pikas

Rabbits are sometimes mistakenly described as rodents. They do indeed have features in common with rats and squirrels, most notably the sharp front teeth that are built to nibble. However, rabbits are just one part of a wider mammal order called *Lagomorpha*. The lagomorphs also include hares and jackrabbits, which are often mistaken for rabbits, but are bigger and distinctly less cute. There are 33 species in all, combining with the rabbits to form the Leporidae family. Hares and jackrabbits (a chiefly American term) are longer-limbed than wild rabbit species. This size advantage also brings a speed boost, and in places where large predators are now long gone,

hares and jackrabbits are among the fastest animals on land. Most can top 70km/h (43mph) over short bursts. Hares do not burrow, but rest in forms, or shallow depressions scraped in the ground.

The lagomorphs contains a second family, called the Ochotonidae. This group contains the 29 pika species. Pikas look too cute to be true, plump fur-balls with passing rabbit features. They are mostly found in the arid rocky regions of eastern Asia, but two of the species also live in North America. Most cannot burrow into stony ground, so make their homes in rocky crevices. A minority of burrowing pikas live in swamps, steppes and meadows.

OPPOSITE:
African savannah hare
This is the most widespread native lagomorph in Africa, ranging from the Atlantic coast of the Sahara Desert, through the Sahel grasslands to the savannahs of East and southern Africa. The hare does not, however, penetrate into the dense jungles of the Congo region.

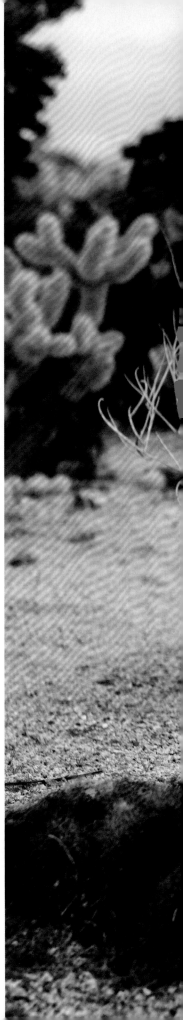

ABOVE:
Cactus eater
Antelope jackrabbits are able to survive in the arid Mexican desert by eating cacti and yucca plants. These plants store a supply of water inside their succulent stems and leaves.

RIGHT:
Black-tailed jackrabbit
This hare belongs to the North American desert and is found in all dry habitats west of the Mississippi, across northern Mexico and along the West Coast up to the border with Canada.

Stay alert
Black-tailed jackrabbits are largely antisocial and solitary, but may flock together around good supplies of food during dry spells. Here one hare has taken an alert posture, standing up on its back legs to peer just that bit further towards possible danger.

OPPOSITE AND ABOVE:

Brown hare

The European hare is also known simply as the brown hare. It is the species that typifies the 'mad March hare' when males are seen to race around fields and engage in short-lived boxing matches over mates and territory. These are also the countryside creatures that link 'bunnies' to the spring festival of Easter.

OVERLEAF (ALL PHOTOGRAPHS):

Cape hare

Also known as the African brown hare, this species lives close to the African savannah hare but is more likely to occupy drier, semi-desert habitats. It is probably the fastest-running hare species, being able to hit 77km/h (48mph) as it zigzags away from threats. Its big ears are filled with blood vessels that shed heat during these great exertions.

White-sided jackrabbit
Chiefly a Mexican species, although a small population extends over into New Mexico, this hare is named after the pale belly fur that extends from the foreleg to the tail. It lives in the high plains and flat-topped tablelands of central Mexico, where winter temperatures can drop below freezing. With a limited range, this species is now in decline.

ALL PHOTOGRAPHS:

Arctic hare
This species is built for life on the polar tundra of the High Arctic and the icy maritime regions of eastern Canada. As a result it is one of the biggest hares of all, topping out at around 70cm (27.5in) long. It is common for cold-adapted species to be larger because it makes the body more efficient. The hare's extremities, most notably the ears and snout, are smaller and more rounded to reduce the chances of frostbite. The tail is almost invisible among the long woolly winter fur. This species is bright white all over except for black tips to the ears.

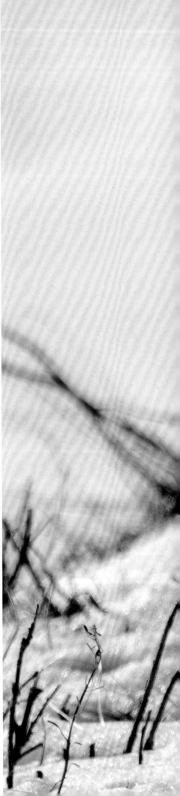

Nowhere to hide
An Arctic wolf chases an Arctic
hare across the tundra. This
treeless polar region comes
alive in the short summer, when
the snow and ice melts away
exposing a barren, treeless
landscape. At this time the hare
changes its colour from snow
white to a dirty brown in an
attempt to stay hidden from
hungry predators.

Plumped up
After an intense period of feeding in the summer, by the time the long Arctic winter arrives, the Arctic hare has a body that is 20 per cent fat. This helps provide further insulation under the blanket of hairs, and it also sustains the animal through long periods with little to eat. Unlike most hares – and in common with many rabbits – these hares dig burrows albeit into soft snow to create shelters from the cold.

ABOVE:
Ethiopian hare
Living almost exclusively in
Ethiopia, this hare is found in the
lowland habitats. Its alternative
name is the bush hare.

RIGHT:
Ethiopian highland hare
As its name suggests, this species
lives higher up than the bush
hare. It is most common in the
Bale and Arle Mountains.

ALL PHOTOGRAPHS:

Haring about

Hares are solitary creatures, and the European species is no exception. They will thump their front feet to the ground to urge away other hares. (A tap from the larger back foot is meant as a helpful warning of approaching danger.) In spring, hares will attempt to pair up. Most of these attempts are a mismatch that ends in violence, but eventually the advances of the male are accepted.

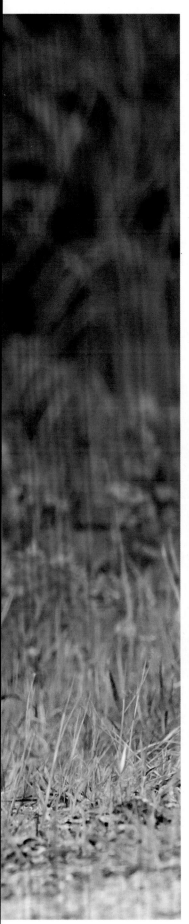

ALL PHOTOGRAPHS:
Granada hare
Perhaps better known as the
Iberian hare because this species
lives across most of Spain and
the southern parts of Portugal,
this is a hare in the literal land
of rabbits. It is most commonly
found in cooler mountainous
habitats, places where burrowing
rabbits could not dominate.

Japanese hare
Found on all mainland islands of the Japanese archipelago except Hokkaido in the north, this medium-sized species has red-brown fur. In the north of its range, some hares will turn white when winter snows arrive.

On the run

A scrub hare is running for its life across the short grassland of the Masai Mara National Reserve in Kenya. Its chance of survival is in the balance because it is being pursued by the world's fastest runner, a cheetah. Nevertheless, the assailant looks to be young and still learning how to hunt for itself so perhaps this fleet-footed hare will live to nibble another day.

ALL PHOTOGRAPHS:
Snowshoe hare
Often mistaken for the Arctic hare for obvious reasons, this cold-climate hare lives in Alaska and the high mountains of eastern North America far to the south of the Arctic Ocean. The winters here are cold and full of snow, although much shorter than in a polar climate.

Snowshoes
The snowshoe hare is named due
to the width of its large back
feet, which, like a real snowshoe,
spread the animal's weight so it
does not sink into deep snow.
This is a significant advantage
when crossing snowdrifts to get
away from hungry predators that
are left struggling in the snow.

ALL PHOTOGRAPHS:
Afghan pika
Ranging from Iran in the west to Pakistan in the east, this little lagomorph makes its home in dry rocky habitats with sparse vegetation. Unable to burrow into the ground here, pikas make their homes in natural holes among the rocks and take a lot of time furnishing them with freshly cropped grasses.

RIGHT & OPPOSITE BOTTOM:

Alpine Pika

Known for its cinnamon brown fur, this pika species lives in and around the Altai Mountains of Central Asia. Here it feeds on mosses, nuts and leaves.

OPPOSITE TOP:

Forrest's pika

Found in the hills of the eastern Himalayas, this species is believed to dig its own burrows. This is unusual for mountain pikas, which normally make do with nests among the rocks.

OPPOSITE MIDDLE:

Himalayan pika

Found as high as 4000m (13,000ft) up, this pika lives among the tallest peaks on Earth running between Nepal and Tibet, including Mount Everest.

LEFT TOP:

Preparing for winter

The American pika lives in the Rocky Mountains and other ranges in the American West. This one is carrying nesting materials for lining its den. It will replace older linings periodically and add extra for winter. This grass-eating lagomorph also builds up piles of cut grasses that will dry into hay – a valuable source of food in the winter.

LEFT MIDDLE & BOTTOM:

Pika den

An American pika emerges from its den. Its hay pile can be seen next to it. This pika species does not burrow out its own nest but makes one under rocks. It is active during the day and returns to sleep at night.

OPPOSITE:

Blending in

Helped by its small size and rounded body, it is hard to pick out a pika among the broken rocks of its hillside habitat.

Characteristics & Behaviour

A rabbit's life is fraught with danger. As a fast-growing and abundant small herbivore, rabbits are an easy meal for carnivores of medium size upwards. Rabbits need to look out for everything from foxes and owls to bears and lynxes. Danger is never far away. To counter these many threats, rabbits and hares have evolved several behaviours. Most obviously they can run, accelerating from a standing start to full speed in a couple of seconds and then zigzagging away. Most attacks on a rabbit are a failure, but predators will keep trying. Hares and rabbits of all types warn their neighbours of danger by thumping the ground with their back feet. They will scream when attacked too. The wild rabbit has a further defensive ploy. It seldom strays far from its warren and is seconds from cover when the alarm is raised. Living in a colony boosts the chances of danger being spotted, and rabbits will work together to close off burrows and protect the young from weasels, snakes and ferrets that manage to worm their way underground.

A pet rabbit is not to know that it is safe from harm and will remain just as vigilant as a wild one. Pet owners should learn to spot the signs of agitation, minimize loud noises and disconcerting smells, and ensure that their rabbit has what it needs to feel safe and secure.

OPPOSITE:
Digging
Pet rabbits have the same urge to dig as their wild cousins, who are frequently maintaining the warren. Giving a pet rabbit a safe place to dig, such as a sandpit, will reduce damage to flowerbeds and fencing elsewhere in a garden.

On the front foot
Rabbits dig with their front feet, using claws to gouge through soft, well-drained soils. The soil is then flung between the hindlegs, and scattered by kicks from the large back feet.

LEFT:

Territorial dispute
Still with their pale winter coats even after the snows have thawed away, these two mountain hares are figuring out who owns this piece of hillside.

ABOVE:

Mister Angry
Pet rabbits are not always as cute and cuddly as they might look. This rabbit's posture signals anger. Baring of the teeth indicates that it is ready to bite and will very likely do so.

Eastern cottontails
A pair of eastern cottontails play out an elaborate courtship where they face off and take it in turns to leap into the air. This non-burrowing species is solitary and highly territorial. Outside of the spring mating season the rabbits stay out of each other's way.

RIGHT:

Gregarious species

As descendants of European rabbits, pet breeds are gregarious creatures that do best when living in small groups. They are just as happy with those groups containing rabbits or members of another friendly species.

OVERLEAF:

Pet foods

Processed rabbit foods contain the mix of nutrients and fibre that the animals need. In the wild, rabbits are coprophagous, which means they eat their own droppings. The first time through the system, the tough plant foods are only partially digested. Gobbling up slime-coated pellets directing from the anus gives the animal a second go at extracting nutrients. The droppings produced the second time around are the familiar dark spheres.

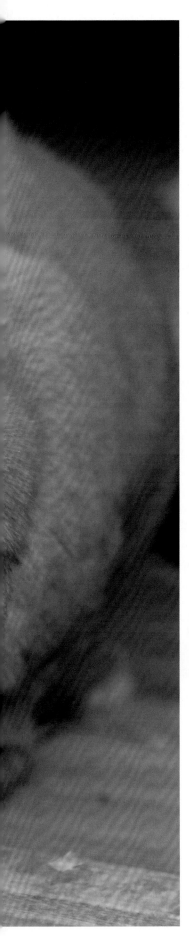

LEFT:
On the nose
This pair of Holland lops look inseparable. Rabbits spend a lot of time communicating with nudges, often with the nose or rump.

ABOVE TOP:
Nudging
A nudge can be used to indicate an invitation to play, or to get attention – and it could be an aggressive act to push the other rabbit away.

ABOVE BOTTOM:
Hiding place
A contented pet, like this giant purebred Flanders rabbit, needs a hiding place close by. The rabbit knows it can retreat to the hutch at any time and so is less stressed by activity and passers-by.

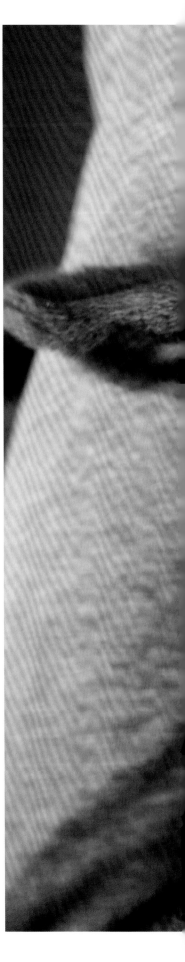

ABOVE:
Eyes half shut
A good sign that a rabbit is happy is when it's eyes are half closed. It will be more open to play, strokes and nuzzles. Get to know your rabbit's moods – they can bite if you misjudge them.

RIGHT:
Back problems
It is increasingly thought that rolling a rabbit onto its back creates stress for the pet. In the wild, a rabbit will only do this in order to play dead for a predator.

ABOVE:
Insect perch
A red admiral seems confident enough to take a perch on this young rabbit's nose. Perhaps it has come to slurp up some salts. The rabbit won't try to eat the insect but there are reports of some wild populations consuming the occasional snail.

RIGHT:
Baby bunny
A young rabbit has a close encounter with its owner. In many ways pet rabbits stay in an immature state when living with people. They are unable to assert dominance using scent markings and aggressive behaviours as they would in a wild warren.

ABOVE TOP:
Multiple mates
While rabbits tend to form monogamous pairings, hares are more promiscuous, with both males and females having several mates throughout the summer.

ABOVE:
Pregnancy
This pet doe will soon be producing a litter of kits. The average rabbit pregnancy lasts about 30 days.

RIGHT:
Growing up
A pair of wild baby desert cottontail rabbits hang out together under a prickly pear cactus. They will soon be living independent of their mother, but have a few months to go before they are fully mature.

Litter mates
This group of rabbit kits look to be around 14 days old. They huddle together for warmth. A normal litter has five or six bunnies and there can be three or four litters a year. Each of these kits could have at least 20 siblings by the end of the year alone.

Ears
Rabbit ears are a defining feature of these creatures. As well as being used for hearing, they also have a role in keeping the animal cool and are used in communication.

LEFT:
Here, hare
At first glance the easiest
feature to differentiate a hare
from a rabbit are its ears. The
hares, and most especially the
jackrabbits, have very long,
oval ears, almost racquet-
shaped in some cases.

RIGHT:
Big ears
These ears belong to a Flemish
Giant, the largest of all domestic
rabbit breeds. They can weigh up
to 10kg (22lb) and the biggest
are 1.3m (4.2ft) long. With a big
body comes big ears. Rabbits are
generally quiet animals but will
scream warnings of attack, growl
at rivals and grunt at friends.

Blood supply
As this image shows, the large ears are filled with blood vessels so they can be used as a radiator to shed unwanted heat. The blood from the animal's hot body is brought close to the surface in the tight skin covering the ears and its heat is stolen away by the breeze.

ALL PHOTOGRAPHS:

Eye colours

A wild rabbit has brown, or less commonly, amber eyes. Domestic breeds have a wider ranger of colours. Rabbits bred for white fur are often albinos and so have red, or ruby, eyes. This colour is from the blood in the iris; there is no pigment at all. Rabbits reared for meat often have red eyes. Blue eyes are very uncommon in the wild but are a popular feature in domestic breeds.

Sideways look
As this picture of a hare shows, lagomorph eyes are on the side of the head so they look to the side of the animal, not to the front. This gives the animals a very wide field of view, almost a full 360°. A hare or a rabbit can therefore see danger coming from any direction but is less able to judge distances than us humans.

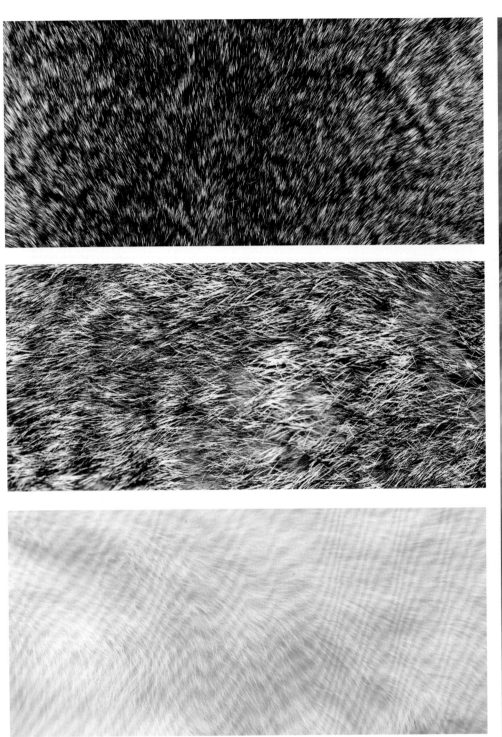

ALL PHOTOGRAPHS ABOVE:

Rabbit fur

Domestic rabbits were originally bred for their fur, which is soft and warm. The coat has a layer of underfur – short, fluffy hairs close to the body that trap a layer of warm air. These are covered by longer guard hairs, which are thicker and oilier. Their function is to keep water off the underfur that would otherwise reduce its insulatory properties.

RIGHT:

Long hairs

Several breeds have developed long hairs. These can be spun into wool yarns or – as is the case with this dwarf rabbit – used to give the animal a distinctive look.

Follow the nose
Rabbits inhabit a world of scent. They have a sharp sense of smell that is 20 times more powerful than humans and rely heavily on it to check for smells that warn of threats such as predators.

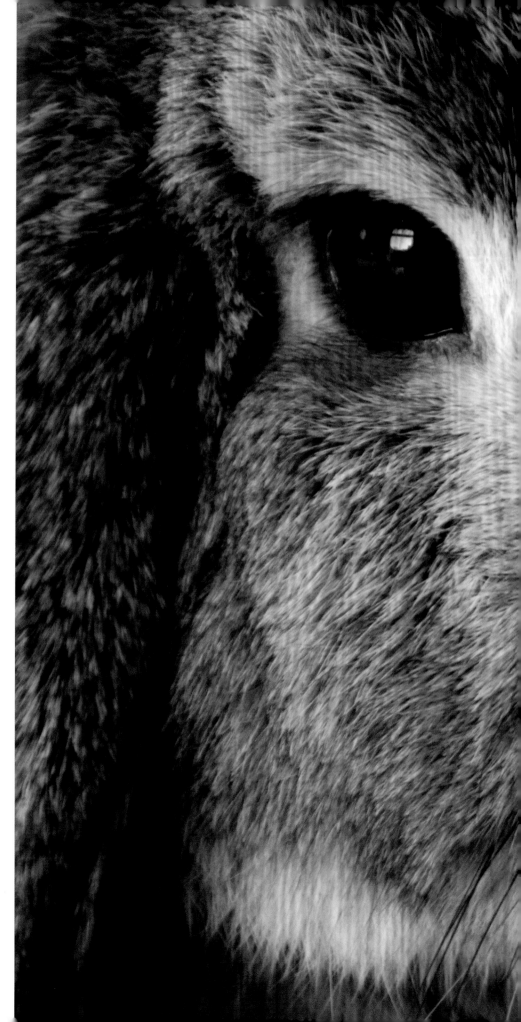

RIGHT:
Front teeth
Rabbits and other lagomorphs have six incisors that never stop growing. Then there is a wide toothless gap, which is ideal for holding bundles of grass and stalks in the mouth.

OVERLEAF (ALL PHOTOGRAPHS):
Chomp and chew
Rabbits use their incisors to slice off a mouth-sized piece of food, including a carrot, that most iconic of rabbit foods. There are a total of 22 premolars and molars at the back of the mouth that grind the tough foods before swallowing.

Rabbit Young

The answer to the question what are rabbits good at is easy: breeding. These little creatures are renowned for reproducing at an alarming speed. The story of the introduction of European rabbits to Australia in the 1780s is especially illustrative. Initially, domestic rabbits were limited mostly to Tasmania, where they were soon noted for becoming a problematic population. However, the mainland infestation has been tracked to the release of about 20 rabbits in 1859 by an English settler in Victoria, who fancied hunting them. In 1866 more than 50,000 rabbits were culled. By 1870 two million rabbits were killed each year, but there was no discernible impact on the population.

Baby European rabbits, better known as kits or kittens rather than bunnies, grow fast, mature young and breed often. Within a month of giving birth, a female is ready to become pregnant again. The kits will have had just one meal a day of her rich, thick milk but that is enough to drive growth so that they can fend for themselves as they enter their second month. At four months they will be sexually mature and near full size.

The same strategy is followed by other lagomorphs – but the communal protection of the burrow means that European rabbit kits are more likely to survive in numbers. Without predators to pick them off, pretty soon these little cuties will be ruling the world.

OPPOSITE:
Never alone
Rabbits are very sociable creatures and seldom find themselves alone. From birth they are surrounded by their kind and so learn to be tolerant of others, including any human family.

Inquisitive
Following a rapid development after birth, baby rabbits begin to be curious about the outside world from about the age of 18 days. However, they are still reliant on their mother for a week or more.

ALL PHOTOGRAPHS:
Breeding like rabbits
Almost before you know it there are more kits – and then more after that. In ideal climate conditions, such as the hills of southern Europe, an adult female rabbit can have five litters per summer with six kits per litter. That is 30 kits, 15 of which will have their own litters the following year. By the autumn of year two, the rabbit population will have grown from two (one female, one male) to 482 rabbits.

ABOVE:
Cottontail
The breeding season for eastern cottontails runs from February to September. This is enough time for kits born early in the season to reach maturity and produce one or even two litters of their own. A quarter of all the cottontail rabbits born each year have parents less than one year old.

RIGHT:
Into the sunshine
The early life of a baby wild rabbit is underground either in a deep warren or a smaller nesting hole commandeered from a woodchuck or other burrowing neighbour. A kit's first forays into the outside world are most likely to be at night.

Invaders
This group of wild rabbits look very much at home sitting outside their warren. However, they are in New Zealand, a remote land famous for having almost no native mammal life, but instead blessed with an amazing community of birds. Rabbits have been causing trouble in New Zealand ever since they were first introduced in the 1830s, using their highly refined breeding ability to spread far and wide. It is estimated that rabbits cost New Zealand over $70 million in crop damage and pest control every year.

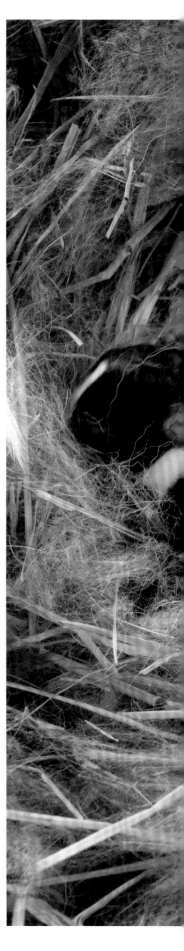

ALL PHOTOGRAPHS:
Early development
Rabbits are born almost hairless and with closed eyes. They huddle for warmth in a nest lined with dry grasses and bird down. The kits are nursed with a rich milk for only a few minutes a day and this is enough to propel a rapid growth. The eyes open on day 11, the ears pop up on day 13 and by day 25 they are nearly 10 times their birth weight.

Sleeping

Rabbits sleep a lot, and mostly during the day. These little kits have opted for an unusual bed. When nursing the kits will have a soft, warm bed to lie on, but the adults flop to the bare ground to sleep. They like to huddle with burrow-mates to stay warm.

OVERLEAF:

Starting out

A pair of little dwarf rabbits take in the summer sun, sitting on the grass. Their life is just beginning. At the age of four months, they will be mature adults.

Picture Credits